DYNAMICS OF DIVERSITY

Strategic Programs for Your Organization

AF644695

Odette Pollar

Rafael González

:50™

A FIFTY-MINUTE™ SERIES BOOK

Viva Books Private Limited

New Delhi • Mumbai • Chennai • Kolkata • Bangalore

Copyright © Crisp Publications, Inc.

First Indian Edition 2004

VIVA BOOKS PRIVATE LIMITED

- 4262/3 Ansari Road, Daryaganj, New Delhi 110 002
  E-mail: viva@vivagroupindia.net
- 215-216 New Apollo Estate, 2nd Floor, Mogra Lane, Andheri (E), Mumbai 400 069
  E-mail: vivamumbai@vivagroupindia.net
- Jamal Fazal Chambers, 26 Greams Road, Chennai 600 006
  E-mail: vivachennai@vivagroupindia.net
- B-103, Jindal Towers, 21/1A/3 Darga Road, Kolkata 700 017
  E-mail: vivakolkata@vivagroupindia.net
- 7 GF, Sovereign Park Apts., 56-58 K.R. Road, Basavanagudi, Bangalore 560 004
  E-mail: vivabangalore@vivagroupindia.net

Published by arrangement with

Crisp Publications, Inc.
1200 Hamilton Court,
Menlo Park
CA 94025
USA

Credits:
Managing Editor: Kathleen Barcos
Editor: Kay Keppler
Layout and Composition: Interface Studio
Cover Design: Nicole Phillips
Artwork: Ralph Mapson

All rights reserved. No part of this book may be reproduced or transmitted in any form or by any means now known or to be invented, electronic or mechanical, including photocopying, recording or by any information storage or retrieval system without written permission from the author or publisher, except for the brief inclusion of quotations in a review.

This edition is licensed for sale in India, Pakistan, Bangladesh, Sri Lanka and Nepal only. Not for export elsewhere.

ISBN 81-7649-554-9

Published by Vinod Vasishtha for Viva Books Private Limited, 4262/3 Ansari Road, Daryaganj, New Delhi 110 002 and printed & bound by Raj Press, R-3 Inderpuri, New Delhi 110 012.

LEARNING OBJECTIVES FOR:

DYNAMICS OF DIVERSITY

The objectives for *Dynamics of Diversity* are listed below. They have been developed to guide you, the reader, to the core issues covered in this book.

Objectives

- ☐ **1) To define the meaning of diversity in the workplace**
- ☐ **2) To show the desirable elements of a diversity training program**
- ☐ **3) To present qualities of good diversity trainers**
- ☐ **4) To present the reasons for diversity training**

Assessing Your Progress

In addition to the learning objectives, Crisp Learning has developed an **assessment** that covers the fundamental information presented in this book. A 25-item, multiple choice and true-false questionnaire allows the reader to evaluate his or her comprehension of the subject matter. To learn how to obtain a copy of this assessment, please call **1-800-442-7477** and ask to speak with a Customer Service Representative.

Assessments should not be used in any employee selection process.

ABOUT THE AUTHORS

Odette Pollar is a nationally known speaker, trainer and consultant to business, government and industry. She is the author of the top-selling book *Organizing Your Workspace: A Guide to Personal Productivity* published by Crisp Publications, Inc.

In 1979, Odette founded Time Management Systems(TMS), a management training firm based in Oakland, California. Odette has worked in public and private agencies, corporations and professional associations. She has trained more than 5,000 professionals in effective time use and organizational techniques. Her clients include Hewlett-Packard, Hitachi America, Beverly Enterprises and Shell Oil. She currently sits on the board of directors for two organizations.

Over the last few years, the Cultural Diversity division of TMS has worked with organizations as they make efforts to increase the diversity of their staffs, vendors and clients.

Rafael González, president of Rafael González Enterprises, has been in business for 15 years, consulting and training all over the United States and internationally. Rafael is a popular keynote speaker and is well known for his dynamic presentations. He has worked with Fortune 500 companies, including Levi Strauss & Co., Chevron, AT&T and Apple. A number of newspaper and broadcasting companies such as Tribune Co., Gannett Co., and McClatchy Newspapers count themselves among his clients, as well as numerous colleges, universities, executive management programs and professional teams such as the Chicago Cubs. In the public sector, Rafael has worked with hundreds of cities, school districts and community agencies; federal, state and local governments; and libraries.

PREFACE

The world is getting smaller. Every year, thousands, even millions, of people leave their native lands and seek new lives elsewhere. This migration has radically altered cultural and economic landscapes, including the work environment, which functions differently than it did as little as 10 years ago.

The new faces and lifestyles have changed how we do business in the 1990s. New customers have created new market niches for products and services. But beyond different marketing strategies, a diverse population will also expand the possibilities of the workplace. It is increasingly common to work with people who act, think, look and respond differently from yourself. Our clients, customers and coworkers are increasingly diverse.

Dynamics of Diversity is written to help individuals, managers, directors, human resource professionals and others who are interested in making changes in their workplace to improve relationships, performance and productivity. For an organization to remain competitive, it must foster a smooth-running, innovative, supportive and profitable multicultural environment. How does your company score on the three Rs? Can it recruit, retain and release the full potential of every employee?

This book provides a step-by-step program for developing a vision for diversity, creating a diversity council to help guide your efforts and developing a training program with strategies for change. It attempts to provide clear and compelling economic reasons for fostering a diverse workplace and shows that multiculturalism can also be fun.

Take this information and adapt it in any way you find useful. Like diversity in the workplace, variety is the spice of life.

Odette Pollar

Rafael González

ACKNOWLEDGMENTS

John Lavine, Joan McCray, Tamara Payne and Thomas Smith, thank you for all your help and support.—RG

I would like to acknowledge Aubrey, Lorie, Richard, Daniel and George for all their help and generosity.—OP

Dedications—

To Stella, Norah, Carlos, Tara and Erica: Thank you for your love.—RG

For my parents, Henry and Mary Ann Pollar, who continue to make all things possible. For Richard Witt, who is a wealth of patience and understanding.—OP

CONTENTS

PART I

An Overview of Diversity

WHERE ARE WE NOW?

Place a checkmark ☑ in the appropriate box. For each "no" or "uncertain," decide what follow-up action to take to change the answer to "yes."

Yes	No	Uncertain	
❑	❑	❑	1. We have conducted a cultural diversity audit.
❑	❑	❑	2. Management communicates information about diversity regularly to its employees.
❑	❑	❑	3. Management is supportive of diversity issues.
❑	❑	❑	4. This organization has a written policy on diversity.
❑	❑	❑	5. There are misunderstandings or problems among different groups and kinds of people.
❑	❑	❑	6. We have identified barriers, issues and problems that employees experience in a multicultural workplace.
❑	❑	❑	7. The financial and personal benefits of diversity have been communicated to employees.
❑	❑	❑	8. We have established an environment where people feel safe to voice their concerns about implementing a diversity program.
❑	❑	❑	9. We have established measurable diversity goals.
❑	❑	❑	10. We understand how to apply diversity concepts to our jobs.

WHAT DIVERSITY IS

Diversity refers to the ways people differ from each other. These ways are significant and there are plenty of them:

- *Culturally*, we vary in:
  - Gender
  - Age
  - Ethnicity
  - Race
  - Sexual orientation
  - Educational background
  - Religion
  - Physical/mental ability
  - Military/veteran status
  - Lifestyle
  - Immigrant status
  - Language facility
- *Functionally*, we vary in the ways we:
  - Think
  - Learn
  - Process information
  - Respond to authority
  - Show respect
  - Reach agreements
- *Historically*, we also vary in:
  - Family make-up
  - Perspective
  - Political outlook
  - Intergroup relationships

So There Are Differences. So What?

When work groups are made up of people with many backgrounds, cultures and lifestyles, promoting teamwork and smooth interactions can be quite a challenge. Finding new ways to work together will require thinking about people's differences–not to divide, separate or exclude, but to take advantage of those differences. We need to create environments that welcome and encourage the benefits of diversity.

Case In Point

Said Barbara Jerich of Honeywell, "We wanted to create a culture that causes women, minorities and people with disabilities to thrive. There are people who also believe it's the right thing to do—morally and socially—but the foundation of the effort is based on a sound business purpose."

START FROM WHERE YOU ARE

Managing diversity is not new. We have all experienced differences that enhance our environment. Every day in your company or organization, you recognize people for their unique talents and skills.

When your computer refuses to cooperate, you turn to a certain coworker for troubleshooting. When someone in the office needs a creative story or an opening joke, they know whom to come to for help. There may even be a closet fashion consultant in your ranks whom you turn to for advice on how you look before you go into a meeting or greet a new client. Differences in skills and talents already exist in your office, and in some ways, you have already learned how to take advantage of them. This is what diversity management is all about.

Beyond computer skills, a sense of humor or a fashion sense, however, the racial, cultural, ethnic and gender differences at work today can cause trouble if they are not handled sensitively. The new aspect about what is variably called "managing cultural diversity," "managing differences" or "multiculturalism," is the quantity and variety of differences in the workforce. Supervisors and coworkers should be careful to interpret cultural behaviors correctly and not give offense where none is intended. Valuable insights may be lost and workers may fall short of their potential if groups or individuals are excluded from decision making. Moreover, cultural insensitivity, in addition to being unproductive, may also be illegal.

WHY DO DIVERSITY NOW?

Work with Changing Demographics

In the United States, the traditional hierarchical, white-male-dominated, large, corporate environment is no longer the norm. By the year 2000, women will be almost two-thirds of all new entrants into the workforce. One out of four people is African-American, Hispanic or Asian-American. Immigrants make up the largest share of the U.S. population increase. There are more people over age 65 than there are teenagers. Ten percent of the population is gay or lesbian.

By learning the new perspectives brought by a wider range of employees, we can provide better services to our clients and customers and to departments within our own organization. New perspectives will enhance our problem-solving skills and allow us to make better and more inclusive decisions. We can learn to ask better questions initially, to identify new areas of opportunity and increase customer satisfaction.

Local, state and federal laws prohibit discrimination based on race, sex, religion and other factors. The laws regarding discrimination require that if a company is found guilty, it must pay damages, all attorney fees and court costs. Millions of dollars are won by plaintiffs every year.

It is counterproductive, however, to expect trouble or fear discrimination suits. Instead, act positively. Treat everyone fairly. Conduct antidiscrimination workshops. Remember, employees are a company's strength. Take advantage of employees' capabilities and perspectives. This will help you provide better services to clients and customers, internally as well as externally.

Enhance Management Skills

The trend in management is away from the autocratic ("I'm the boss. You listen to me and do what I say.") to consensus ("Let's decide this together."). More companies are shifting from a hierarchical structure to individual contributors and teams. This shift requires new skills of communication, negotiation, collaboration and team building. Leaders must orchestrate teams comprised of diverse individuals, and gaining full cooperation from everyone on the team is critical to performance.

DIVERSITY AT HOME

A Personal Checklist

See if your workforce population matches the diversity of the population at large. Consider your workplace multicultural if:

- ☐ One-half of the managers are women.
- ☐ The percentage of minority employees is reflective of your local population mix.
- ☐ There are men and women at all levels and in all positions throughout the organization.

How much do you contribute personally to diversity in the workplace?

- ☐ Do you eat lunch with different people every day?
- ☐ If you can, do you offer special projects or challenges equally to people from different races or language groups?
- ☐ If you can, do you suggest supplemental training equally to all employees?
- ☐ Do you promote employees based solely on their qualifications?
- ☐ Do you try to ensure that no groups of employees are hired only for certain jobs (Asian-Americans in production spots, whites in managerial positions, etc.)?

DIVERSITY AT HOME (continued)

In your opinion:

Yes No

❑ ❑ Given the diverse workforce you have, are you getting the same productivity, level of morale and teamwork that you would get if every person in the company was of the same sex, race and nationality?

❑ ❑ Are the people in your company working at their best?

❑ ❑ Are there any particular groups of people (for example, women, minorities, immigrants, gays or lesbians, older people, or people with disabilities) who have a higher turnover rate than the general population of employees?

❑ ❑ Does management at your organization pursue the goal of a diverse workforce, and are achievements rewarded?

❑ ❑ Does the leadership of your organization express a vision that encourages diversity as a business goal?

❑ ❑ Are diversity issues addressed regularly in program design, policies and company literature?

❑ ❑ Is your leadership skilled in communicating with clients, employees and customers from many backgrounds?

WHY BIG BUSINESS SUPPORTS DIVERSITY

In an effort to recruit and keep top-tier employees of all races and both genders, Fortune 500 companies have begun to address diversity issues in the workplace.

When Avon's sales dropped, the organization began a very aggressive development and recruitment program. Management realized it had not understood the impact of demographic changes—including the effect of women moving into the workplace—which meant fewer women stayed at home to receive the "Avon lady." Said James E. Preston, CEO of Avon: "We understand that managing diversity is not something to do because it's nice, but because it is in our interests."

Lynwood L. Battle of Procter & Gamble said, "We make no apologies for making this a competitive issue. The companies that are going to survive and thrive in the next century are the ones that take full advantage of their workforce."

WHAT CAN I DO?

No matter how large your organization, any person can start the diversity ball rolling. You can:

- ***Learn About Diversity***

  Read articles, books and journals. Keep your ears and eyes open. Attend special events, programs and seminars. Learn about some of the diversity issues faced by others. If you do not understand something about a culture different from your own, ask.

- ***Talk to People***

  What do your colleagues and associates think about your organization and its willingness to address diversity issues? What have they experienced, positively and negatively, about diversity? Keep in mind that a broad definition of diversity includes all types of diversity: age, gender, ethnicity, positions in the organization, education level, immigrant status, seniority, language facility and sexual orientation, to name a few.

- ***Research What Other Companies Are Doing with Diversity***

  Do not reinvent the wheel. Learn what has worked for other companies. This helps avoid time-consuming and costly mistakes. This information will be a powerful tool in advocating for a diversity initiative.

  Mention that although diversity management has social benefits, companies such as Xerox, Hewlett-Packard, Procter & Gamble, Levi Strauss, Honeywell, Digital Equipment Corporation, McDonald's, and Avon have embraced diversity management for economic reasons.

- ***Involve the Human Resource Department***

  What do your company's formal statements say about how it does business? Are any direct references made to diversity? It is easier to build support and find funding when a company is formally committed to diversity.

  If no such statements exist, look for complementary programs that will provide an initial jump start. (Quality committees, employee-involvement committees, customer service initiatives, senior executive meetings are examples.)

  Make sure that you are familiar with what your company has already done in related areas, such as sexual harassment. If these programs have been successful in the past, knowing what worked well and building on those successes will help get your program off the ground. Then develop a report outlining your findings. Include the costs and benefits of diversity initiatives. However, as an individual with many responsibilities, you will need help in gathering information, doing research and developing strategy. The human resource department can help guide your efforts.

- ***Develop a Resource List***

  Begin to compile a resource library on diversity. Start a clipping file from newspapers and periodicals. This can be a relatively safe way of learning about the subject, particularly for hesitant or skeptical employees. It can act as a source of additional information for those who want to move ahead quickly or who have a pressing concern. Videos, books, and articles can also be a great low-cost resource for ongoing discussions. Plus, the information will keep visibility and momentum going for diversity efforts.

Any Person Can Start the Diversity Ball Rolling—Even You!

BUT I AM ONLY ONE PERSON, OR ONE DEPARTMENT

Starting a diversity effort is not a quick, easy process. This does not mean that a single person cannot make a difference, but it does mean that you will have to be clear about your role, limitations and resources. You can continue to be involved in the process over the long haul while still getting your regular work done. Once you have started the diversity ball rolling, your role will be one of support and strategic planning. Here are some of the things you can do:

- Provide services to a diversity committee (teach meeting-facilitation techniques or offer meeting space at your location).
- Be responsible for initial logistics and meeting reports until the steering committee or task force develops its structure.
- Clarify how much you and your department will be involved in the diversity process.
- Provide information on your department's demographics.
- Ensure that all employee groups are involved, including union shop stewards and employees from administration, clerical, maintenance and housekeeping. All information must be shared.

You might be only one person in the company, but one person can have a very large effect. Think of yourself as a pebble tossed into a pond. The pebble may be small, but the ripples it creates get bigger and bigger until they splash on the shore, sometimes miles away.

EEO, AA AND DIVERSITY: WHAT'S THE DIFFERENCE?

One of the most common misconceptions about diversity is that it is really only Affirmative Action (AA) or Equal Employment Opportunity (EEO) with a new name. Although this is not true, EEO, AA and diversity efforts are not mutually exclusive and can ideally support one another. Outlining the differences will be critical in getting people to respond positively.

EEO and Affirmative Action serve *social* purposes. Diversity management, on the other hand, serves *economic* purposes. Diversity management differs in purpose, approach, character and scope.

EEO and Affirmative Action were designed to eliminate barriers certain groups faced and combat racism and prejudice in hiring practices. In defending against prejudice, EEO denied differences among people. Being different was equated with being inferior. Therefore, equal rights came to mean that everyone is to be treated the same, with equal access and opportunity.

Many organizations found that meeting affirmative action hiring goals was possible. The difficulty was in retention, particularly in management. One of the factors contributing to the poor retention rate was that success for individuals different than those in the mainstream was based on how able the person was to fit in, or assimilate. His or her difference was downplayed or often ignored entirely. This was a high price for many individuals to pay and the result was a high turnover rate.

Diversity management suggests that success be based less on assimilation and more on inclusion, differences and all. The goal is to seek out and encourage the new perspectives and approaches to situations that different employees bring to work.

Diversity management is designed to increase productivity and profitability in businesses and organizations. Unlike EEO and Affirmative Action, it is fueled by economic concerns rather than primarily legal or moral concerns.

To value and capitalize on the differences people bring to their work, organizations must be willing to make whatever changes are necessary—systems, rules, procedures, management practices—that unintentionally give certain people advantages over others.

WHAT'S THE DIFFERENCE? (continued)

Diversity management is different from Equal Employment Opportunity and Affirmative Action in purpose, approach, character and scope:

TWO SIDES OF A COIN

EEO and Affirmative Action	Diversity Management
• Social purposes.	• Economic purposes.
• Fueled by legal or moral concerns.	• Fueled by "good business."
• Designed to combat racism and prejudice in hiring practices.	• Designed to increase productivity and profitability in businesses and organizations.
• Reactive. Sets recruitment hiring goals and monitors compliance.	• Proactive. Uses a variety of tools, programs, procedures and strategies to maximize each person's contributions.
• Set up to overcome barriers certain groups faced due to racism, prejudice, and bias.	• Looks at the current situation and moves forward to make the most of it.
• Being different traditionally seen as mark of inferiority.	• Leaders realize being "different" does not mean "inferior." Different is normal.
• Equal rights means everyone is treated the same.	• Realizes that different people value different rewards.
• Denies differences among people.	• Confronts reality of differences and acknowledges them.
• Differences became sore points or problem areas.	• Values differences and strives to turn them into advantages by translating them into a company's assets.

Diversity Management is Just Good Management of a Heterogeneous Workforce!

WHY SOME DIVERSITY PROGRAMS FAIL

Diversity efforts are change efforts. Change suggests uncertainty and even disruption, and thus many people have a difficult time in coping with and understanding change. Assumptions about the process can discourage, derail or prevent success even before you design your diversity initiative, let alone implement it.

You will have to identify, examine and confront assumptions about who should be involved and who should lead the initiative, who should be trained and who is responsible for monitoring progress, what needs to be changed and how to go about doing so. These assumptions can be deeply ingrained, and many companies have difficulty getting started. The following are some common problems.

SEVEN REASONS FOR FAILURE

1. COMMUNICATIONS BREAKDOWN
2. UNREALISTIC EXPECTATIONS
3. THE TRAINING HAS FOCUS BUT NO STRATEGY
4. IT IS TOO EXPENSIVE
5. ANOTHER PROGRAM THAT COMES AND GOES
6. FAILURE TO COMMIT
7. REVERSE DISCRIMINATION

#1: COMMUNICATIONS BREAKDOWN

The Problem

When an organization changes the way it does something, the new procedures are often accompanied by confusion and misinformation. Many strategies for change have failed because of poor communication, raging rumors and few opportunities for discussion.

The Solution

Establish a way to communicate at all levels of your organization, across all lines and up and down the company ladder. Develop this early in the process so you can share information and ideas, answer questions and receive critical feedback.

Use the corporate communication methods that are already available throughout your organization: newsletters, electronic mail, memos and informal "water cooler" talks. To find out whether the system is working, ask. You may need to establish a separate communication vehicle just to discuss diversity. For example, General Electric Nuclear Energy decided to sponsor a multicultural fair, which was very successful. It was filmed and used as an innovative way to communicate to the whole organization about diversity efforts.

#2: UNREALISTIC EXPECTATIONS

The Problem

Sometimes companies are too impatient. Major cultural changes take time, and diversity initiatives are major cultural changes. Task-driven, results-oriented, short-term thinking all prevent long-term success for almost any strategic process. Unrealistic expectations can result in failure to create and sustain long-term change.

The Solution

Develop a plan that includes short-term goals, thus ensuring that you will have early successes. Meanwhile, design a strategy for long-term goals and actions. The short-term objectives and tasks are the building blocks for the long-term goals.

#3: THE TRAINING HAS FOCUS BUT NO STRATEGY

The Problem

The organization means well. The managers want to include everybody, but they forgot the vision, mission, tasks and timing needed to make up a complete strategy. This approach assumes that diversity issues can be "solved" if you just try training, which can lead quickly to a marketplace search for a suitable program. However, change is a process, not a program. If employees feel that "this is just another training program," or "this is just corporate politics," you are fighting an uphill battle.

The Solution

Do not keep your plan a secret. Let people know about the diversity vision, mission, tasks and timing—your strategy. If you analyze how the training fits into the overall organizational culture, strategy and beliefs, you can avoid undermining other initiatives or training programs. Diversity training can complement these other efforts.

Publicize the objectives of the diversity training, which may reveal opportunities employees did not know about before. You may also discover potential conflicts with the timing of other work projects.

#4: IT IS TOO EXPENSIVE

The Problem

Executives want to make employees happy, but usually they want that happiness to be achieved at no cost to the company. Managers may consider employees' individuality and interests, but then, prematurely, they ask, "What's the bottom line?"

The Solution

Make sure that almost every time you talk about diversity or have a training or evaluation, you mention the business rationale behind it: the advantages it gives your company competitively; your strategic plan, diversity's values and principles and market opportunities. Discuss how implementing a diversity program can be inexpensive, especially when compared to other programs. And a bargain when compared to the cost of not implementing it.

#5: ANOTHER PROGRAM THAT COMES AND GOES

The Problem

Employees may not be enthusiastic about the diversity program. They may be judging by what they have seen before: the way the company handled other ideas, initiatives or programs—big effort one month, no follow-up the next. Or they may be used to being "th last to know" about major organizational changes.

The Solution

Someone other than a human resources person should lead the diversity council o steering committee, which will help break old patterns of letting the diversity effort be an "HR thing." If you include people throughout the company, you will point the organization in the right direction: of taking responsibility and developing the commitment, skills and abilities that will help the diversity proces evolve.

Include employees in as much of the process design, planning and implementatio as possible. Tell them (and show them!) that their insights are important. Encourage participation in your assessment process. Establish an interested guiding group, council or committee. Make sure employees participate in pilot training sessions.

Offer to share diversity perspectives and learnings that are supported by existing training programs (for instance informational and behavioral interviewing skills, coaching, or supervisory training), which reinforce that diversity is a way of doin business, not just another training course.

#6: FAILURE TO COMMIT

The Problem

Too often, executives are monitors. They remove themselves from the process, asking that everyone else make the changes without being willing to lead the way by example. Sometimes employees interpret this as leadership lacking in commitment and sincerity. Employees may be guarded and suspicious. They may question managers' integrity.

The Solution

Change does not happen simply because of an edict from the top. Leadership clearly must support change, both in writing and action. Managers need to spell out their diversity values and guiding principles. They need to make people aware that they expect everyone to evolve, grow and change, including themselves. They can most prove their commitment by practicing what they preach and by integrating a diversity perspective into all arenas. For example, Avon encourages employees to organize into African-American, Hispanic and Asian-American networks by granting them official recognition and providing a senior manager to act as mentor. At least once each year, James E. Preston meets with each employee group.

#7: REVERSE DISCRIMINATION

The Problem

Diversity efforts tend to focus on ethnic or racially identified groups, which makes it easy for European-Americans and men to say, "This is for everybody else but me." Leaders may then avoid confronting those employees' beliefs. Instead, they pay attention to employees who are more sympathetic or who more easily identify with the diversity effort.

The Solution

Emphasize that the diversity effort is a learning process that includes everybody. Everyone's insights are important, especially employees who have been at the company a long time. Value their experience. They have decision-making ability and power. Help them realize it is for the sake of competitiveness, customer service and quality. Keep the lines of communication open and keep everyone in the loop. Remind all people that discrimination is illegal.

INVOLVING SENIOR MANAGEMENT

Senior management's commitment is a key factor in any diversity project. Management must be made aware of the strategic, competitive and bottom-line benefits of valuing diversity. There are several ways to gain senior management support.

1. **Start Out on the Right Foot.**

   Involve senior management in the effort early on. Ask them to play a key role when it comes to supporting and making a visible commitment to the effort. Involving them early will help them work through common questions and dilemmas so they can be clear about their participation and expectations.

2. **Cite the Competition.**

   If senior management is not committed to diversity, educate them about the value of diversity to business. Do some research on the diversity practices and successes of other companies in your industry and let management know about these successes.

3. **Uncover New Market Opportunities.**

   Enlist the aid of marketing to help develop an information program for management. Include culture-specific market analyses of various population segments and highlight the advantages of broadening the business base to include these diverse groups.

Case In Point

One Fortune 500 company's manufacturing division had very little senior level commitment. The company had employee problems that were affecting the bottom line: absenteeism, poor productivity, etc. They formed a committee. The goal was to analyze the problems and recommend solutions. One of the key recommendations was a "valuing diversity" training. It started at the senior levels and was offered throughout the organization. This training addressed specific problems raised by employees and managers. The effort was very successful.

PROMOTE DIVERSITY TO IMPROVE MORALE AND PRODUCTIVITY

When employees are overlooked or ignored, morale is low. People want to feel that they are important and that their contribution matters. Recognizing and using people's abilities and experiences involves them in a way that builds rapport, respect, ownership and loyalty. The higher morale is, the harder employees are likely to work and better productivity results.

Toward this goal, employees seek answers to the following questions:

- How attractive does the company look to people who do not fit the mainstream?
- Do I feel welcome and comfortable being myself?
- Am I encouraged and allowed to work to my full potential?
- Am I rewarded for my work and allowed to share in the decision making?
- Do I fit in?

Observations About Diversity In My Organization

____

____

____

____

Things That I Would Like To See Change

____

____

____

____

HOW ORGANIZATIONS BENEFIT FROM DIVERSITY

Businesses receive many benefits by recognizing and encouraging work force diversity. Among the many benefits, consider the economic impact of these top three:

1. **Tapping into the Tremendous Purchasing Power**
   - Older Americans spend over $800 billion annually
   - Minority markets buy more goods and services than any country that trades with the United States
   - Understanding different values and perspectives opens new markets

2. **Reducing Costs by Reducing Employee Turnover**
   - Highly trained workers will stay with organizations that are responsive to their needs
   - Retraining is expensive
   - High employee turnover reduces morale and productivity

3. **Receiving the Benefits of Productivity, Creativity and Innovation from All Employees**
   - New perspectives enhance problem solving
   - Business success is often dependent on group performance
   - An inclusive environment builds respect, ownership and loyalty

Remember: If you do not capitalize on the benefits of diversity, your competitors will!

Case In Point

As part of their early work in diversity, one Fortune 500 computer company identified success stories that happened because they value diversity. They also shared experiences where a lack of diversity awareness lead to loss of revenue or higher operating costs.

P A R T II

Implementing a Five-Step Diversity Training Process

STEP 1: START WITH A VISION OF DIVERSITY

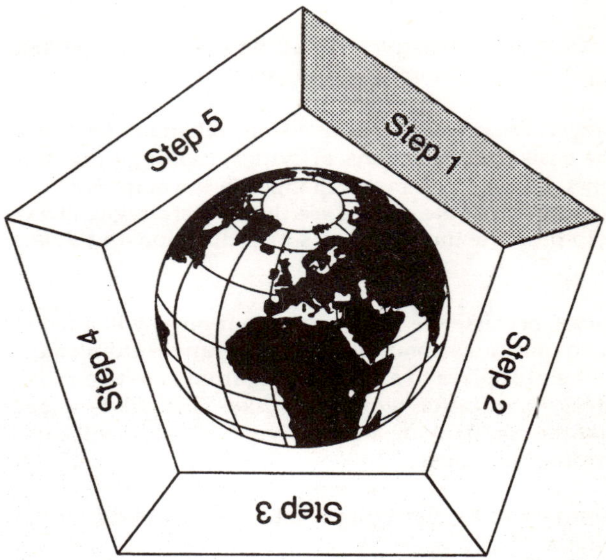

It is important to start with a vision and mission. Without a clear plan, the diversity initiative may be confusing or lack strategic direction. Initiatives trapped in this quagmire ultimately have a limited effect or, worse, a negative one. Many companies get caught up in activities. Without a clear vision and mission, activities can lead to a trivialization of the attitudes the company wants to promote, which can create a backlash toward the whole effort.

WHAT THE VISION STATEMENT CAN DO

A diversity vision statement is valuable in several ways. It will help you to:

1. ***Wrestle with tough questions,*** including individual understanding of, and organizational commitment to, diversity.

2. ***Keep on target,*** because a diversity vision statement becomes the goal and the basis for any actions, activities, training programs or special events. If you recommend changes in the employee evaluation process, people should see this as a strategic intervention that will help promote the company's overall vision and diversity mission.

3. ***Provide focus,*** because the vision statement gives you a focus for responding to questions about why the company is doing a diversity initiative. A helpful place to start building from is to use a vision of what the ideal organization would look like. This will help people discuss what the company means by diversity and how it can affect the "bottom-line" outcome.

4. ***Build a foundation*** by clarifying what you need to do for the diversity effort.

Case In Point

Levi Strauss & Co. developed an Aspirations Statement that captured its organizational and cultural philosophy. They based a major training effort on this philosophy, teaching their employees about their priniciples and values. They created diversity training and strategies under that philosophy's umbrella.

DIVERSITY VISIONING

There are many ways to develop a diversity vision. Here are guidelines that can contribute to a successful process.

The Diversity-Visioning Process Should:

- Involve as many people in the organization as possible. Ask a cross-section of employees to react to the diversity vision. Some companies ask a small, representative group of employees to develop the vision and then share it with senior management and the rest of the employees for feedback.

- Include opportunities to discuss personal and organizational visions, which allow people to voice a range of perspectives. You can use the information later to identify where visions are similar and analyze how to build momentum and support for the diversity effort.

- Conclude with a document that is communicated throughout the organization. You can use the final diversity vision in training programs and to check diversity strategies to ensure that they are in line with the vision.

- Reflect the core principles and values the organization has identified.

Sample Vision

"To create a work environment that emphasizes our commitment to treating each other with dignity, trust and respect by recognizing each others' beliefs, values and differences."
(General Electric Diversity Council, 1993)

QUIZ

1. How well do I understand diversity issues (social, legal, moral, economic, practical) affecting employees and customers?

____

____

2. What principles and values does my company promote organizationally?

____

____

3. How does this diversity vision relate to any existing company-wide vision statement?

____

____

4. What is our common understanding and definition of diversity?

____

____

5. What areas of interest and personal agendas do we have that may influence the vision—and our approach?

____

____

6. What building blocks does this company have in place to help us begin a diversity initiative?

____

____

STEP 2: CONDUCT A CULTURAL AUDIT

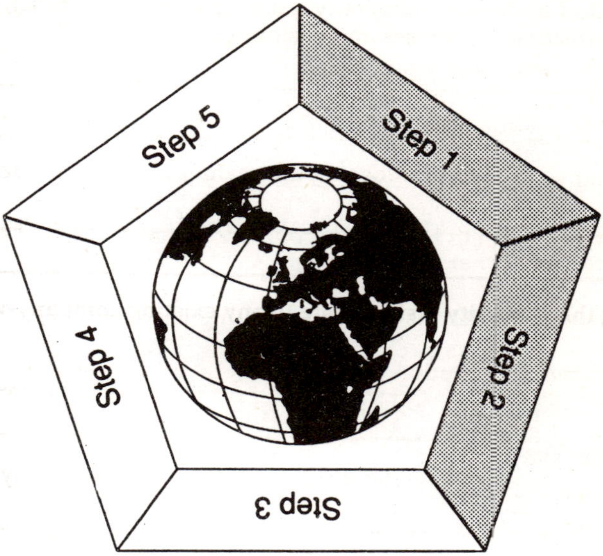

Accurate, useful and timely background information is critical in building a strong foundation for diversity efforts. It will help you make sound decisions when you design a training program. An audit is one strategy for gathering information from a large or dispersed population.

The cultural audit, when properly designed and carried out, identifies the organization's strengths, climate, issues, understanding, obstacles, challenges and possible starting points for a strategic diversity initiative. An audit does not stop being useful after a training program has begun. As your diversity program continues, use it to monitor and measure progress.

AUDIT GOALS FOR YOUR ORGANIZATION

√ Provide an overview of your climate for diversity

√ Provide information on the dynamics of diversity among employees

√ Understand issues and concerns about diversity

√ Provide information to leaders and trainers to make sure that diversity is integrated into other endeavors

√ Find out how diversity fits into your existing vision and mission

√ Provide critical information for leadership

Avoid These Traps

Be cautious of three common traps into which audits, surveys and other large data gathering endeavors fail:

1. The data gathering itself becomes the solution: "See, we did a survey."

2. The process becomes an academic exercise—the information is not used until it has been polished into an acceptable form, which can take months or years.

3. The survey serves only as a one-way information-gathering tool. When doing a cultural audit, allow this to be a two-way communication. Take this opportunity to *give* information about your plans, mission and vision.

Analysis is important, but do not deliberate in silence. Keep ideas, conversation and interest alive. Avoid months of silence followed by a massive ad campaign to unveil the results.

A SUCCESSFUL CULTURAL AUDIT

Information gathered in the cultural audit should:

- Cover a broad range of issues from many viewpoints.
- Show how diversity stands now and suggest directions and actions for the future.
- Include a broad spectrum of people throughout the process.
- Be positioned in a positive light.
- Be gathered by diverse interviewers. Consider using an outside organization. Employees will feel that there is more confidentiality between data collection/summary and presentation. Outside interviewers can also be more objective during interviews.
- Include both qualitative (focus groups and interviews) and quantitative (survey results) data.

Benefits of a Cultural Audit

- Provides empirical data
- Helps identify what training and incentives employees need for professional and personal development
- Provides information, so trainers and human resources staff can better coordinate all development programs
- Identifies perceived barriers, issues and problems that employees experience in a multicultural work environment
- Uses sound information to develop action plans and strategies for valuing diversity in the workplace
- Identifies strength and support for diversity in the organization

HOW IS A CULTURAL AUDIT DIFFERENT?

A cultural audit is different from a traditional organizational survey in several ways:

Traditional Survey	Cultural Audit
Focuses on organizational climate in general.	Focuses on organization's climate regarding diversity.
Often limited in the number of groups isolated for comparison and analysis.	Allows a broader number of groups to be isolated for comparison and analysis.
Rarely asks specific questions to isolated groups.	Includes specific questions related to isolated groups.
Often initiated by human resources, top management, rarely committee driven.	Often initiated by Diversity Steering Committee, other employee groups, as well as human resources.
Focus groups are often limited to function, site, department or level.	Focus groups include a wide variety of groups and includes race, gender, age, and disability.
Is primarily a data collection tool.	Is both a data collection tool and a way of educating employees. Assists in designing training programs.

Before You Start

There are several questions you should ask yourself when you are planning to do a cultural audit:

- Is this a good time to do an audit?
- What worked well and what has not?
- How will we use the information?
- How will we comunicate the results?
- What is the role of the senior executive?
- Is there support for an audit?
- What support do we need?
- How have we done past surveys?
- What information do we want?
- What will it cost?
- What should the human resources role be?
- What about others in the organization?
- How will we guarantee confidentiality?
- Who will sponsor the audit?

THE AUDIT, STEP BY STEP

Action	Date Begun	Date Completed	Results
Prepare written rationale			
Get support from senior managers			
Design a proposal			
Prepare a strategy to communicate the results			
Develop success criteria			
Identify measurable goals			
Conduct the audit			
Analyze the data			
Communicate the results			
Evaluate the impact of your audit			
Identify the next action steps			

DESIGN A COMPREHENSIVE CULTURAL AUDIT

For a comprehensive and accurate cultural audit, use four techniques:

1. The Inventory Survey

This written survey should be tailored to your organization's culture and needs. Its main purpose is to generate data useful in developing your diversity strategic plan. The survey is effective because it allows people to remain anonymous. Give it to a cross-section of employees or, if time and resources permit, to the total organization.

2. Focus Groups

Develop focus groups, each of which should have four to six people from your organization. Each group should have a similarity, such as older employees, night shift workers, women, etc. This approach shows how groups view a common set of questions or experiences a situation. Start the group by asking an open-ended question (those that encourage more than "yes"or "no"answers). You can be guided in choosing which questions to ask by what you discover in the written survey, which allows you to corroborate data and gives you a deeper understanding of some of the organizational issues that may influence responses to the survey questions.

3. Individual Interviews

You might want to probe more deeply and find out how people perceive and define diversity in the organization. Interview a diverse sampling of your organization. Allow 30 minutes for each one-on-one interview and ask open-ended questions.

4. Consultant, Vendor or Customer Observations

A vendor from outside your organization, or sometimes clients, can give you objective data based solely on their observations while working within the organization. This perspective will be quite valuable.

If you carry it out and analyze it well, a cultural audit will give you concrete information on many areas: the diversity issues facing your organization, obstacles or resistance you are likely to meet, what is going well and suggestions for some next steps.

SAMPLE DIVERSITY INVENTORY SURVEY

> NOTE: To elicit feelings and observations, questions should be open-ended, not answerable with only a yes or no. Encourage people to express themselves honestly.
>
> **Remember: An audit should be custom designed for each organization.**

1. Would knowing more about how different kinds of people live and think help you work better with them? ❑ Yes ❑ No

2. When it comes to your day-to-day environment, how well do you feel your company values the following groups? Check 0 for not at all through 4 for very great.

	Not At All 0	*Little* 1	*Some* 2	*Great* 3	*Very Great* 4
White	❑	❑	❑	❑	❑
Asian-Americans	❑	❑	❑	❑	❑
Women	❑	❑	❑	❑	❑
African-American/Blacks	❑	❑	❑	❑	❑
Disabled	❑	❑	❑	❑	❑
Men	❑	❑	❑	❑	❑
Hispanics	❑	❑	❑	❑	❑
Religious Minorities	❑	❑	❑	❑	❑
Gays/Lesbians	❑	❑	❑	❑	❑
Native-Americans	❑	❑	❑	❑	❑
Recent Immigrants	❑	❑	❑	❑	❑
Pacific Islanders	❑	❑	❑	❑	❑
Older than 40 years old	❑	❑	❑	❑	❑
Others (please list ________)	❑	❑	❑	❑	❑

3. How would you rate your company's commitment to diversity?

0	1	2	3	4
❑	❑	❑	❑	❑

4. How well do you feel your company nurtures or mentors the following groups when it comes to professional development? Check 0 for not at all through 4 for very great.

	Not At All 0	*Little* 1	*Some* 2	*Great* 3	*Very Great* 4
White	❑	❑	❑	❑	❑
Asian-Americans	❑	❑	❑	❑	❑
Women	❑	❑	❑	❑	❑
African-American/Blacks	❑	❑	❑	❑	❑
Disabled	❑	❑	❑	❑	❑
Men	❑	❑	❑	❑	❑
Hispanics	❑	❑	❑	❑	❑
Religious Minorities	❑	❑	❑	❑	❑
Gays/Lesbians	❑	❑	❑	❑	❑
Native-Americans	❑	❑	❑	❑	❑
Recent Immigrants	❑	❑	❑	❑	❑
Pacific Islanders	❑	❑	❑	❑	❑
Older than 40 years old	❑	❑	❑	❑	❑
Others (please list ________)	❑	❑	❑	❑	❑

5. Do you believe that our organization has fair policies toward its employees?

____

6. On a day-to-day basis, are you treated fairly?

____

7. Do you feel you get the support you need to be a better employee and make progress in your career?

____

8. What kinds of problems or misunderstandings have you seen occur among different groups and kinds of people?

____

9. Do you believe that any group of people here is deliberately or unconsciously discriminated against in any way? If so, how?

____

10. What could we do differently to get everybody to participate 100%? What would this organization or facility be like?

____

11. What would be a significant milestone that would show that we had made real progress in managing diversity?

____

12. What do you like best about working here?

____

13. What is the one thing that you would change?

____

14. What is your company doing well in the area of diversity?

____

15. What are your concerns about your company's diversity initiative?

____

16. What could your company do to increase the respect and encouragement of diversity in your work environment?

____

17. What could you do individually to support a valuing-diversity initiative in your organization?

____

INTERVIEW FOLLOW-UP QUESTIONS

NOTE: If you elect to offer a portion of the Diversity Inventory Survey as an oral interview, use the following questions as guidelines to get a more complete answer to the participant's responses.

1. How often does that happen?
2. Can you give me an example or two?
3. Can you tell me some more about that?
4. Do you believe it happens to you or others?
5. Tell me the story about how that occurred. What happened?
6. When that happened, what did it mean to you?
7. What other problems are you having with . . .?
8. What opportunities/possibilities do you see in . . .?

Optional Background Information

This section is for statistical purposes only and will be used by the task force to study how different groups of people view this organization's diversity. We do not want your name, but would appreciate the following information.

1. ____ Male
   ____ Female
2. __________ Race
3. __________ Department
4. __________ Position
5. What is your age?
   ____ Under 25
   ____ 25 to 35
   ____ 35 to 50
   ____ Over 50
6. How long have you been with this company?
   ____ Less than 1 year
   ____ 2 to 5 years
   ____ 5 to 10 years
   ____ Longer than 10 years

STEP 3: FORM A DIVERSITY TASK FORCE

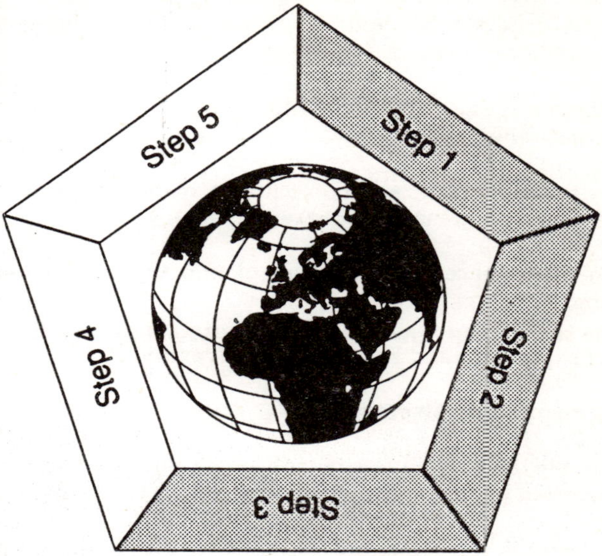

For any diversity effort to be successful, your organization needs to have vitality, power and a commitment to make changes. Some very important questions can help you focus your thinking on these issues.

- How can you include the entire organization?
- Who will organize or lead the effort?
- Who will help smooth the process?
- What is the best way to continue?
- How will we use the information?

To provide leadership, focus and continuity, consider forming a task force to study, organize and direct your diversity effort. The traditional starting point for diversity efforts is often in the human resources and training departments. Even though they are not solely responsible for all the work, these departments will have key leadership roles.

FORMING THE TASK FORCE

Involve a broad cross-section in choosing membership in the task force. Consider several criteria when you pick members for a diversity task force. People on it should represent different:

√ Races, gender, ages, sexual orientation, physical abilities, political orientations, religions, etc.

√ Levels within the organization (executives, managers, secretaries, housekeeping, maintenance, nonexempt, etc.)

√ Departments (finance, line managers, plant managers, customer services, marketing, etc.)

√ Levels of experience and knowledge of diversity

You can help ensure this diversity by:

√ Widely publicizing the diversity task force's purpose and focus. That way, interested people or groups have a chance to get involved.

√ Telling everyone about the process for assigning committee membership. Make it fair and open. Make sure your communications invite ideas and comments.

√ Explaining what type of ideal representation the committee should have. This is true whether the membership process is by appointment, nomination or volunteering.

√ Publicizing who the committee members are.

√ Being flexible.

The selection process should not be final until you have received feedback about the proposed members. For example, if there are no Asian-American members, or no one from a field location, make changes. If there is still no representation from a particular group, move forward with your plan, but continue to reach out to the groups to encourage future involvement.

Once formed, the task force should rotate members. New people bring new perspectives, ideas and energy to the group, which helps avoid burn-out for members.

Task Force Responsibilities

1. *Clarify Roles and Expectations* Ask senior management to play a key supporting role. Clarify their expectations and find out how much decision-making power and resources are available.

2. *Get to Know Each Other* Get task-force members to talk about their reasons for being involved, their vision of diversity, and their current challenges in this area.

3. *Determine the Mission and Vision* Establish the mission and vision of the task force. Early in the process, communicate the beliefs, values and mission statement to the rest of the organization.

4. *Get Educated* Identify additional training needs, including managing change, diversity awareness, conflict resolution, facilitation skills and cross-cultural communication.

5. *Benchmark* Identify best practices, document successes and target potential future strategies.

6. *Gather Data* The cultural audit can be used to collect information about the current climate for diversity and any building blocks that support it.

7. *Divide into Subcommittees* To make the most of time and resources, split the task force into subcommittees. This allows multiple areas to be worked on simultaneously.

8. *Determine the Communication Strategies* Reach out to all departments to involve them in the diversity process. This is a good time to seek out those departments that are not very enthusiastic about change.

9. *Share Your Progress* Do not be modest. Brag about the successes. Keep people updated, interested and excited. This builds and keeps momentum.

10. *Lay Out the Budget* Your strategic plan should include an annual budget to sponsor special events, pay for outside consultants, or acquire needed training materials. You need money to fund a year's worth of specific activities or purchases.

THE FIRST MEETING

The first meeting is a critical one. Consider using a good facilitator, either from inside the company or an outside consultant. During that meeting you will find that people have a wide range of concerns. Even if all the participants feel knowledgeable about the issues, there will be many assumptions and perceptions of what a diversity effort is all about. You will need to address them.

Concerns	Ways To Respond
1. *Is senior management really committed to this effort?*	1. Offer any written examples of commitment. Show a video of the CEO discussing the importance of diversity. Ideally, have a senior executive present.
2. *What is the connection to business?*	2. Provide the financial rationale, show figures from other organizations.
3. *How safe and open will the committee be? Will it be easy to discuss diversity issues?*	3. Have members share their life histories and self-interests. This helps to create an environment of honesty, community and directness.
4. *How effective will this group be?*	4. Have individuals share cultural norms and individual needs.
5. *What is the scope of the work the committee will do? Will the committee be able to lead a diversity effort?*	5. Help allay worry by exploring and clarifying the committee's role and mission and then communicating it to the organization.
6. *How will emotional issues be handled?*	6. Discuss personal safety. Set ground rules for confidentiality—for example, not having personal issues made public. Explain that the outcomes and decisions however, should not be kept secret.

First Meeting: Sample Agenda

Welcome, Meeting Objectives, and Agenda

Senior Executive Brief Presentations:

- "How diversity is tied to strategic business direction."
- What diversity is and is not.
- Questions and answers.

Who Are We?

- Members share brief life history and include their personal reasons for being diversity task force members.

Group Cultural Norms:

- Each member shares how he or she works most effectively.
- Each member shares concerns that might present obstacles in being an effective member of the diversity task force.

Define Roles and Mission:

- Group explores its potential role and mission as a leadership committee.

Stay on Track

The task force should focus most of its time and energy on devising a strategy for the diversity initiative. The strategy should connect the diversity initiative with other business goals. Use existing organizational structures and business processes to support the diversity initiative. When you implement new programs, create support structures, including financial support, appropriate evaluation criteria and reward systems.

Early Task Force Meetings: Issues To Address

There are several objectives for the early task force meetings. These can be broken down into clear, specific and measurable goals. It might take several meetings to address the following issues. Consider these to be the foundation of the task force. Try to address each of these tasks as early in the process as possible.

Early Agenda Issues

Have senior executives share their statements of commitment.

Tie business strategies to the diversity initiative by using an executive report.

Develop the committee's roles and expectations.

Clarify and share individual member's self-interests, motivations and needs.

Provide members with diversity training.

Brainstorm potential actions for next steps.

Clarify the criteria for setting priorities on potential actions.

Identify members' issues and concerns.

Set up meeting protocol and structure.

Develop a list of organizational building blocks and obstacles.

Establish subcommittees to develop action plans, measurements and time lines.

Develop the vision and mission statements.

Future Agenda Issues

Develop communication vehicles.

Get additional diversity, leadership or other group-process training.

Prepare a business plan and budget.

Have subcommittees report on their progress.

Develop a method for measuring and monitoring progress.

Assess the organizational strategy.

Carry out subcommittee work.

Prepare and share a progress report for senior executives and employees.

Begin to use organizational communication tools to spread the word and involve other business units.

Develop a best-practices document to include:

- internal examples within your industry
- outstanding examples outside of your industry

THE ROLE OF HUMAN RESOURCES

The human resource manager who works with diversity issues will be in a leadership position. This job requires many roles, including:

CATALYST

Finding and developing opportunities and resources to gain support, increase credibility and reinforce diversity efforts.

RESEARCHER

You need a solid base if your organization is developing a diversity initiative from scratch. You need comprehensive information. Gather organizational statistics and examples of diversity initiatives at other companies. Then summarize and condense the data into a usable form and share it with employees, managers, the training department and senior executives.

ADVOCATE

Some organizations hesitate to allot time and resources for a diversity initiative, perhaps because they don't understand diversity or fear the cost of implementing a program. You may have to spend a lot of time outlining why the company needs to develop a diversity initiative, and what benefits it could gain from doing so.

PROBLEM SOLVER

Be familiar with successful intervention strategies for creative problem solving. Examples are finding funding sources, helping make sure staff has time allowed for attending meetings and identifying key players.

FACILITATOR

Be a person who makes things easier. Implementing a diversity initiative can bring up issues, concerns and discussions that pose challenging situations even for experts. For example, many people do not have skills and experience in communicating across cultures or genders. Your organization may ask you to be a facilitator and moderate those discussions, demonstrate communication techniques, create positive experiences for people struggling with difficult diversity issues, and open channels of safe communication.

INFLUENCER

You may need to provide resources to influence decision makers. Learn your organization's politics and be aware of the system's structures, which can create both opportunities and obstacles for a diversity initiative. Constantly measure how much support employees demonstrate for the initiative. Notice what their needs are. Use this assessment to develop partnerships, share resources and develop constituencies that will support the diversity initiative.

SUPPORTER

Support the efforts and programs of others. Trust them to help and participate.

STRATEGIC THINKER

Do not sacrifice long-term strategies for short-term goals. Early in diversity planning, organizations commonly focus on visible, short-term efforts—for instance, a celebration of Women's History Month. Those efforts are fine as far as they go, but as the strategic thinker, make sure that your organization also uses energy and resources on longer-term strategies that will affect the way the company does business. Long-term strategies include changing internal structures and processes that determine reward systems, performance appraisals and the focus of business-development strategies.

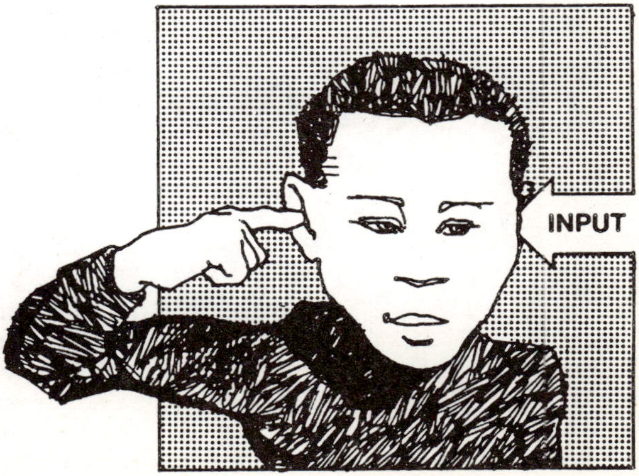

What Your Role Should Not Be

- **The sole person responsible**—Do not try to be "Super Diversity Leader." If you are the only person driving the initiative it will be very difficult to keep the program alive.

- **The primary focus of the diversity strategy**—You and your department should not be the only focus of the diversity initiative. Diversity is a business issue, so address it in all areas of your organization.

- **A problem creator**—Unfortunately, some professionals can create obstacles, conflict and problems for an organization through lack of knowledge and expertise. You should be aware of your own strengths and weaknesses and make sure you seek out expertise in areas that are uncomfortable or unfamiliar. Trouble is assured if the professional:
  - √ has a political axe to grind
  - √ tries to use a diversity initiative to become famous
  - √ has a hidden personal agenda
  - √ tries to push for their own group's interest
  - √ uses diversity for personal gain

Be Neutral and Inclusive of Everyone

STEP 4: DESIGN A DIVERSITY TRAINING PROGRAM

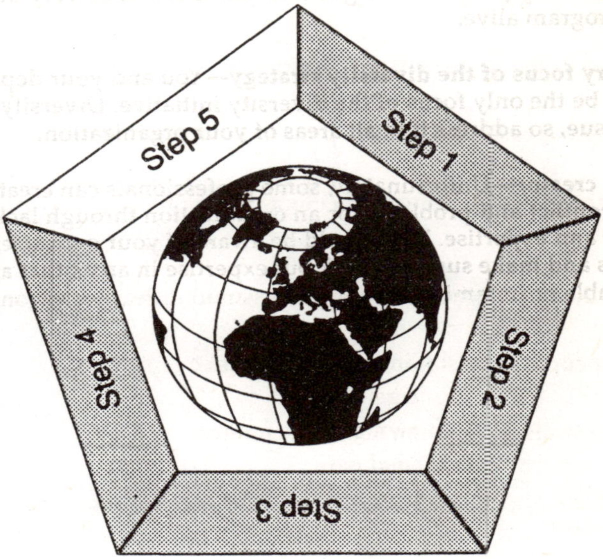

If there were a Hall of Fame for diversity training complaints, there would be two top winners:

1. The training is too "touchy-feely." It lacks focus.

2. The training was "great," but nothing has changed. There was no real impact.

Although training alone should not be your sole strategy, it can anchor a diversity program. When a business begins using any new technology—a new software system or new machinery—it is easy to measure success. Can employees use the technology effectively? Can they apply it in a way that makes doing business easier, quicker, more productive or more profitable?

The same should be true with diversity. You need to give employees and managers the tools needed to make diversity work for them and for the business. Any diversity training should answer these questions.

- What is diversity?
- How does diversity benefit the workplace?
- What challenges does diversity present to employees and managers?
- What is the effect of changing demographics on our workforce, markets and communities?
- What is likely to happen if we bring diversity into a work group?
- Why do people have stereotypes and biases?
- How do antidiscrimination laws affect me?
- What are the organization's policies, goals and expectations for diversity?
- What are the skills that each person needs to be successful in a multicultural environment? How can I use diversity to my advantage?
- How do I apply these concepts to my job?

DIVERSITY TRAINING BASICS

TRAINING DESIGN BASICS

IDENTIFY NEEDS

Examine issues from the human resources viewpoint. Why does this subject interest you? What have you observed at work? Have you received complaints or heard comments from employees? The comments might be, "I can't cope with so many people who are from other countries. Some of them can't even speak English!" or "Young people have no work ethic!" Your observations might come from noticing that the older employees are not asked to participate in company events. Or perhaps most of the line staff is multicultural, but their managers are not. Or maybe there is a disproportionate turnover of women in upper management.

These observations made by you and others are important because they serve as a starting point for discussion. However, there are other issues and concerns that you may not have heard yet from employees. This is why using the results of a cultural audit is important.

DESIGN THE COURSE

1. Identify the extent of the training. Examples include a program that:

- Can be offered throughout the organization
- Is easy to understand and fosters cooperation
- Is portable—can be used at different sites
- Is not threatening, confrontational or blame-oriented

2. Review any existing programs that would have an impact on your diversity initiative. Examples include hiring policies and procedures (are they inclusive and expansive?), performance review policies (do they support diversity efforts?), sexual harassment policies or training (is the message clear and consistent throughout?), Americans with Disabilities Act (how has the company responded?), etc.

3. Take the issues identified in the cultural audit. Set priorities on the issues identified. The most pressing or critical issues are the ones to focus on (for example, legal practices or equity and fairness concerns). Keep in mind that no matter how many issues your research might identify, you cannot do everything at once. Change, particularly changes to the way a system works, is a continuous, long-term process. Allow the diversity training process to occur in stages.

4. Design a course to meet your needs. Choose the media involved, the exercises and the trainers.

5. Determine how you will measure your effectiveness. What pre- and post-training measurements would allow you to evaluate success?

6. Start with a pilot program. Take the comments about the session as a basis for redesign. This feedback mechanism should be more than just a simple evaluation form. The pilot group should give you reactions to exercise choices, film selection, language use, instructor ability and overall usefulness.

7. Make any revisions necessary.

8. Offer the course to the entire employee group.

9. Evaluate the success of the program.

OTHER COURSE DESIGN CONSIDERATIONS

Although lecturing has its place, much of the high-impact, thought-provoking portions of diversity training come from hands-on participatory or experiential learning. When designing a course, facts and figures alone are not enough.

Lecture	Interactive Learning
• Does not seek out a variety of opinions or perspectives	• Allows participants to express their views
• Participants sit still and listen; it is a one-way transfer of information	• Creates opportunities for participants to exercise their own skills in managing diversity discussions—promotes two-way exchanges of information
• Most effective with large groups	• Most effective with smaller groups

Experiential learning is the adult learning model. Adults learn best when they can participate in their learning process, build on their own experiences and have fun. Using this style in diversity work makes attendees more vested in the program's success. It can go a long way in defusing anxiety, resistance or hostility.

CHOOSING EXERCISES

Make your exercises inclusive. Do your exercises include:

Yes	No		Yes	No	
❑	❑	Cultural differences	❑	❑	Conflict resolution
❑	❑	Change cycles	❑	❑	Nonverbal communication
❑	❑	Intercultural communication	❑	❑	Information on bias and stereotyping
❑	❑	Employee development	❑	❑	Workforce make up and trends
❑	❑	Cross-cultural training			

FIND YOUR FOCUS

The focus of diversity trainings vary, but it usually falls under one or more of four areas: cognition, behavior, emotion or organization.

Cognition

This approach to diversity training provides information, statistics and data. Participants learn facts and figures, such as laws governing fair employment practices, how to understand data, how we categorize and form stereotypes, changing workforce demographics and changes in the customer base.

For example, the trainer might make the following statements:

- Almost one in every four Americans is black, Hispanic or Asian.
- In the next 10 years, ethnic and racial minorities will grow seven times faster than whites.
- People with disabilities make up the largest minority: 45 million people.
- The population is aging: people over 65 outnumber teenagers.

Behavior

This approach to diversity training provides concrete behavioral examples. It is rather similar to the childhood game "Simon Says." Participants practice skills through role plays, case studies or simulation exercises.

This type of training is helpful because participants need clear guidelines on what "valuing diversity" language and behavior looks and sounds like.

For example, the trainer might use such case studies as:

CASE STUDY EXAMPLE #1

The supervisor of a production team has just retired. He has been replaced by a 30-year-old man with only two years experience, but a strong educational background in production management and quality. All of the other members of the production team are at least 10 years older than he. You are introducing him to the group at a team meeting. How can you help to ensure his success as a supervisor?

CASE STUDY EXAMPLE #2

There are three people on a project team.

The most senior member consistently does good, but not outstanding, work. He gets along well with his peers. His seniority carries a lot of weight, which means he has many contacts that prove useful to the team.

The second team member is a people person. Of all the team members, he produces the least measurable work, but his ability to work the system and build relationships with people were the reasons why the team's work got noticed by the task force.

The third member is the "brains" behind the work. She is very quiet and not very comfortable speaking in front of people.

A special task force has requested that one member of the project team give a presentation about his or her latest work. This opportunity would offer a lot of visibility and be a great career enhancer for the one chosen to be the presenter.

You are the one to make the choice. What are the issues you would consider? Whom would you choose? Why?

Emotion

This approach to diversity training provides a challenge to participants: It makes them examine their own deep-seated, sometimes unconcious reactions to difference.

We all have personal prejudices and stereotypes. Organizations can benefit from employees being made more aware of how people perpetuate exclusion and prejudice.

> **STEREOTYPE AWARENESS EXERCISE**
>
> Place a group of eight volunteers in a circle. Give each one a card on which has been printed a word (leader, blabbermouth, tentative, ignore me, shy, interrupter, silent, know-it-all). Have each person wear a sign, but not read it. They must discuss some issue given to them by the trainer. Each person must treat the others in the group according to what his or her sign says. The rest of the class watches the interaction without making comment. At the end of the exercise, solicit reactions first from the group of eight. Then let them see what their signs said and compare what the observers noticed with what the volunteers felt.

Organizations that want to discuss the emotional issues of diversity must be extremely careful to find experienced and well-qualified facilitators. Hire or choose your diversity professional with great care.

Organization

This approach to diversity training lets you examine your organization's structure and processes. For example, the trainer might help you examine reward systems, development programs and performance appraisal systems. These systems and processes should support diversity. If a company thinks diversity is an important business issue, managers should evaluate employees on their participation in diversity programs. If a company values parenting or the physically challenged, it will have a parental leave program, elevators and accessible bathrooms.

Teams can find ways to include new members and support their learning and early success. The organization can look at who it might be excluding from information loops and what effect this has. An organization that wants to benefit from a diversity initiative has to incorporate this focus in its training.

Any of these approaches will make a difference if it is done well. The more approaches taken by an organization, the better. Each approach will support and complement the others.

DO NOT GET LOST

Pitfalls are frequently asked questions that trainers can get stuck on. Some trap questions such as, "Why are people the way they are?" have no answers at all. Here are some examples and some handy suggestions for responses.

Tricky Question	Response
Is diversity only for minorities and women?	Diversity includes all people. It involves many dimensions of difference and is much broader than race and gender. It can include age, position, education and immigrant status to name a few. Diversity is an inclusive term that allows us to recognize that both differences and similarities play a big role in business success.
What does this have to do with the bottom line?	Diversity is always about two things: principles and values on one hand, and business success on the other. By drawing on different perspectives, you can increase innovation and understand your customers and employees better. (Provide specific examples from your organization of how diversity can aid business.)
I only see human beings; I see no race or gender.	It is important to recognize both similarities and differences that all human beings have. To ignore the fact that an individual is a particular race or gender is to deny a key part of that person. We are not all the same. The important step is to move past what is visibly different or similar and to discover new aspects of people so that you can better understand them.
This is like EEO—just about numbers.	Diversity is different from EEO or Affirmative Action. It is a long-term strategy, which focuses on key business principles: developing new market niches, improving customer service and making a better quality work life for all people.

DIVERSITY TRAINING IS UNIQUE

Training is not easy work. It requires empathy, process skills, knowledge of learning styles—not to mention content expertise. After building a solid base of technical training skills and following years of experience in supervisory, management and leadership training, trainers can add new programs to their repertoire with little difficulty.

Diversity training is different. Even if you have been delivering programs successfully for years, diversity training requires extra skills, which are in many ways more important than learning the new program content.

Diversity training differs significantly from training in other human resource issues in 10 ways.

1. ***Emotions rear their heads.*** Diversity issues tap directly into peoples' emotions. Responses to questions, comments, exercises and information will often be emotionally tinted. The emotions will vary from person to person and run deeper than the emotional response likely to be exhibited in, for example, a time-management class.

   This is not a one-way street. As the instructor, you are not immune or distanced from your emotions during the training program. You must manage your emotions while paying attention to what is going on in the room.

2. ***Money makes the world go round.*** Whether it is right or wrong, most business decisions are based on economics. Participants must see the diversity initiative tied directly to business success. Emphasis should be placed on the economic impact of diversity issues, the role that diversity issues will play in decision making and ways that a diversity approach creates business opportunities.

   Tying training to business goals is always important; however, diversity training will fail if you do not make this connection, and make it often. Bolster the connection to a business rationale with statistics or anecdotal data from your department, company, or organization. If that information is not available, trainers should provide relevant examples of diversity's business impacts on other companies and industries.

3. ***Open their eyes.*** Unlike other programs that can begin with behavior change or skill building, diversity training must begin with awareness. A primary goal of diversity training is to help people be more open, aware, sensitive and empathetic. To reduce bias and be more flexible and understanding, we must first identify our assumptions and understand how those affect our perceptions, which in turn affect situations we face daily.

4. ***Do not allow wallflowers.*** To be consistent with its very name, diversity training requires the inclusion of *all* people. Make an extra effort to encourage participation from everyone in the session. Remember, however, that participants will have a range of participation *styles*. Do not demand that everyone be outspoken and upfront, for example, but do not let people be totally silent. Be sensitive to your language choice, tone, nonverbal cues, pacing, presentation style and exercise design. This will help create an environment where people can express feelings. In the same vein, do not ask the sole Latino or Asian in a group to speak for the entire ethnic population.

5. ***You have to get personal.*** Examining personal responses to differences is critical in diversity training. For some people, personal experiences about diversity and differences quickly tap into emotions. Issues that come to the surface are not always neat, tidy or controlled.

   It is critical to remember that *all* experience is valid. It is your challenge to make sure you address singular, unpopular or uncomfortable experiences with skill and sensitivity. Do not gloss them over or subtly dismiss them. It is very common for an outwardly similar group of people to have very different and often contradictory experiences. For the participants, there are no right or wrong responses.

6. ***Practice what you preach.*** The trainers themselves must model diversity. Diversity training gives the message that inclusion, reaching out, variety and difference are all important. Same-type trainers (i.e., all male, all black, all the same age, etc.) give off an inconsistent message. Having trainers who are different from each other is an excellent way to model that styles and ability differences can and do work smoothly together.

7. ***Be a tour guide, not the know-it-all.*** The diversity trainer is more of a facilitator and a guide than an expert. The expertise needed in diversity is less on content, although that is very important, than on having skills in group dynamics, processing problems, building safe environments, being personally vulnerable, counseling and negotiation.

8. ***Show it in the best light.*** Positioning the diversity initiative within the organization is crucial to its long-term success. It must be viewed as a permanent business commitment in which all employees will participate and from which they will all benefit.

9. ***We are all in this together.*** Diversity initiatives need cross-organizational support from departments, different levels in the hierarchy and individuals. A diversity effort is less likely to succeed if viewed as only a women's or minority initiative.

10. ***Keep the ball rolling.*** Diversity training is not a one-time event. Like safety, it works only if you use it every day.

Case In Point

One Fortune 500 Company arranged for a meeting with the training department, leaders of the quality initiative, and the strategic business planning committee. These three groups shared their goals, their future plans, and talked about areas where they could use support. They then planned ways to integrate the three initiatives. This allowed them to be more supportive, effective and use resources more efficiently. This process helped the organization present a united, integrated, well thought-out plan rather than a series of disconnected initiatives.

REVIEW

DIVERSITY TRAINING IS UNIQUE	SPECIAL TRAINING SKILLS NEEDED
• Highly emotional	• Be able to manage your own feelings
• Behavior change is not always immediate	• Make the environment safe for all participants
• Needs to be tied to economic factors	• Be highly skilled at group process
• Requires that both trainer and trainee get personal	• Be aware of your own biases
• Requires that trainers be diverse	• Be comfortable with what you do not know
• Switches from content expert trainer stance to facilitator	• Have highly polished design skills
• Must position the training before, during and after a program	• Be flexible
• Requires cross-organizational support	• Know your organization well
• Is not a one-time event	

COFACILITATION ENHANCES THE TRAINING

Cofacilitation, which models teamwork, is a very effective approach for diversity training.

Opposites Attract

It is great to pair up trainers who are different in some visible dimension: physical ability, race, age, gender, etc. If that is not possible, different styles (extrovert/introvert or formal/informal) can also give participants opportunities for learning that differences can complement and benefit a team.

Some work environments do not appear to have a lot of diversity. Diversity is often interpreted as having cultural, ethnic or racial variety; however diversity has other dimensions including age, sexual orientation, physical ability, language facility, etc. In those situations especially, diverse training team members can provide a very powerful learning experience for participants. They model equal, respectful and effective relationships.

The Dynamic Duo Conquers Challenges

Two facilitators can also be helpful if a conversation becomes difficult or hard to manage. Discussions about diversity can be very emotional. They challenge our own picture of the world. Resolving the embarrassment and frustration of diversity "misunderstandings" can be uncomfortable.

If a few participants pull one cofacilitator into a discussion or argument, the partner can balance the roles by monitoring the larger group reactions and comments. Even in nonvolatile situations, one facilitator can focus on group process, monitor time and track learning points. This leaves the other free to engage the group in discussions and activities.

THINGS TRAINER TEAMS HAVE TO WATCH FOR

- ***Becoming blabbermouths.***

  Two facilitators should *never* talk twice as much as one facilitator. Participants should never have to fight for "air time" with the facilitators.

- ***Finding too much strength in numbers.***

  Participants should not feel overwhelmed.

- ***Assuming you know what the other is thinking.***

  Being cofacilitators is a lot like being spouses. You can get in trouble if you assume you know what the other facilitator wants or needs. Talk about delivery styles, what each of you does well, what your challenges are, what kind of support you like from a cofacilitator. That way, you are less likely to have unresolved issues or miscommunications. You can use your skills and styles to complement each other.

Model an Equal, Respectful and Effective Relationship

STEP 5: TRAIN PEOPLE TO TRAIN

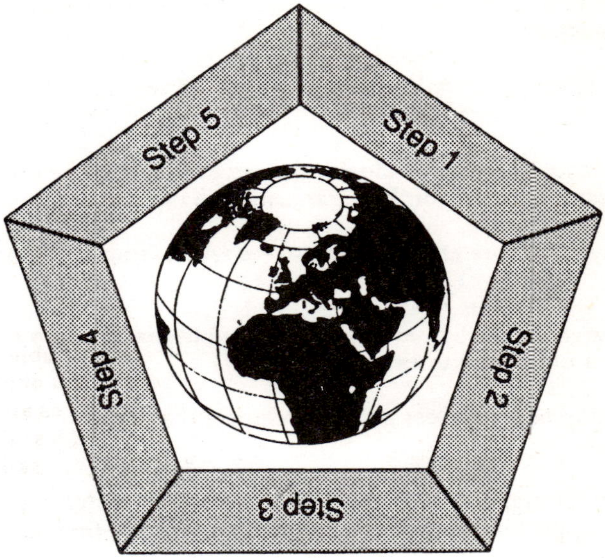

The challenge facing many companies is the desire to include all employees in training. Yet the time and costs for that can be prohibitive.

Training trainers is one strategy for increasing direct involvement of employees and a method to train a larger group of employees very economically. It lets you develop an internal core group of trainers who can multiply the impact of the training department. In addition to training, the trainers can facilitate discussions related to diversity issues and provide informed leadership in the diversity effort.

BENEFITS

- Trainers gain new skills and knowledge that they can contribute to other change efforts.
- Trainers can tailor presentations based on their knowledge of the department, division or unit.
- Trained employees become a valuable resource in leading the diversity effort by engaging the rest of the organization in discussions.
- The company has a core group of employees who exemplify diversity principles.
- Companies save money by providing training internally, and it avoids burnout of training department staff.
- A diverse group of employees gains development and networking opportunities.
- The visibility throughout the organization can be very helpful in promotional opportunities, project assignments or cross-functional team selections.
- A resource center initially created to help trainers can be made available to the entire organization.

As an internal diversity trainer, you can:

- Be actively involved in the diversity effort.
- Lead training sessions.
- Make sure there is continuity and provide appropriate training throughout the diversity effort.
- Be a valuable resource for information and direction as the organization moves toward creating an environment that truly values diversity.
- Facilitate discussions on diversity.
- Provide help to managers wanting to learn more about diversity and its application to the work force.
- Support and encourage diversity even when away from the classroom.

COSTS

- Employees and their departments' need to invest time.
- One-time costs for trainers' workshops, resources and materials.
- The employees best suited to participate as trainers may be involved in other projects.

SELECTION CRITERIA

The selection criteria for participation can include both qualitative and quantitative elements.

Quantitative	Qualitative
• How much experience candidates have in training and in making presentations. • Diversity-related training candidates have already participated in. • Demonstrated leadership skills in diversity. • Knowledge based on reading and experience. • Time and availability.	• The training team should be as diverse as possible (function, race, gender, age, experience). • Individuals should be interested in diversity. When asked, they should be able to put their interest—and commitment—into words. • An employee who could benefit from the opportunity for professional development.

THE TRAINING OF TRAINERS

Trainers need time to learn the content of this new program. In addition, a session needs to include a self-awareness component, design component, practice time and ample opportunity for comments and discussion.

GET TO KNOW YOURSELF

The self-awareness component helps explore one's own culture and biases. Diversity trainers need to be able to use their life experiences as catalysts for learning, and they need tools to cope with their own emotions.

LEARN ABOUT DIVERSITY

Trainers need to understand the stresses in diversity training. They need strategies for handling tough situations and ways to help the participants manage their emotions.

LAY OUT YOUR PLANS

The design component of your training allows you to relate your training to business goals and strategies. The trainer must know the basic elements of a diversity design, including what to expect from participants and how groups function.

PRACTICE MAKES PERFECT

The practice component is very important. Practice conducting the program, including delivering and receiving input by videotape, in writing and by oral feedback.

Develop an Internal Core of Trainers

DO NOT:

√ Be drawn into areas outside your understanding.

√ Handle EEO or supervisory issues that should be referred to the appropriate channels.

√ Give legal advice.

√ Overestimate your limits, both personal and organizational. You need to be able to explain those limits to others.

√ Be the only expert. Your role should be primarily a facilitator. Being labeled as a know-it-all can block the dialogue that is so important for learning.

√ Do everyone else's work.

√ Do things you are not ready for. The effective diversity trainers know what they do not know.

If you are asked to do a class on a particular cultural group and you have no knowledge or experiences with the group, do not offer the session yourself; find a resource to present this class.

√ Try to do too much.

√ Underprepare. Know your audience. Know your material. Make sure you take care of all logistics before training. Explain your role before and during the training. Clarify the group's expectations and set a realistic agenda.

THE ULTIMATE DIVERSITY TRAINER

A swimming instructor does not have to be excellent in the butterfly stroke to teach the stroke to others, but that is not to say swimming instructors do not have to know what they are doing in the water. The following is a list of personal development areas for diversity training.

Be Self-Aware and Able to Manage Your Own Feelings

Diversity issues are emotional. We all carry biases. The more aware we are of our own, the more effective we can be in helping people see theirs.

Trainers must be comfortable being uncomfortable. Stirring emotions is the only predictable thing in this training. Being continually surprised is the norm. Not all of what the session leader experiences will be fun, pleasant or comfortable. Being able to feel the discomfort and still manage the session takes an extra level of skill.

Be Able to Make the Environment Safe

The environment must be safe enough for others to feel able to express experiences that they do not normally share in a group. Part of building this safe environment involves knowing when and how to use confrontation to protect members of the group. Because confrontations will occur, setting standards for effective challenges is important. Particularly when discussing biases, stereotypes and assumptions, it is critical that you stop inappropriate behavior. Turn a potentially explosive or divisive outburst into a learning opportunity for the entire group.

Be Good with Group Dynamics

The trainer who creates an environment in which the group members can talk meaningfully is much more likely to have a successful session. Adult learners need practical information that allows them to build on their experience and provides them with some control over the learning environment. This is especially true of diversity training because of the confusing experiences and feelings that people bring to the session.

The trainer must understand the developmental stages of groups. When groups evolve, disagreement and confrontation with the leader are often signs of progress. The surface manifestations of excessive politeness and tentativeness may in fact be a sign of trouble.

Be Comfortable with What You Do Not Know

No single person can be an expert on every area within the diversity arena. No one can know all about the Americans with Disabilities Act, gay and lesbian issues, all about the various cultures in Southeast Asia, what African-Americans want, how women truly feel, what Hispanics face in the United States, what it is like being an immigrant, the problems faced by the physically and mentally challenged or what Vietnam vets experienced. Draw on the experiences within the group to learn from.

This is another reason that having diverse trainers is necessary. Each brings a different expertise and set of experiences that helps the program move forward.

Have Highly Polished Design Skills

People have many learning styles, ways of showing respect, responding to authority and interacting in a group setting. You must have sophisticated skills to design a program that allows space for everyone to be comfortable and participate. Do not be surprised if after piloting the session, you have to redesign the session.

Be Very Flexible

No matter how much planning goes into the design, you cannot predict which issues will arise. Trainers must be able to make snap decisions and change in midstream when the need arises. Some opportunities are too good to let pass, and being able to redesign a segment quickly is important.

Know the Organization, Its Norms, Culture and Style

Your organization will determine how you design and position a program and whom you enlist to your cause. Identify the structures, procedures or policies that will support diversity efforts, which are not always directly related to human resources or the training department—for example, justification for the initiative may come from a new product being developed in engineering.

What are the concerns, pressing issues or hot spots? Introduce the initiative in stages or phases. What issues make the most sense strategically to tackle early on? For what projects does your organization allocate resources and which program is it likely to fund? Do you need to address specific concerns to build a solid foundation for later work? Do not stop marketing the program after you introduce the first set of courses. Positioning is important before, during and after the session.

Bringing It All Together

Each manager and trainer will bring unique skills and qualities to the training. Management's job is to blend these individual styles into an effective training format and demonstrate how the information will benefit the employees and the organization. The training goals should be both measurable and attainable. Effective training is good for everyone—it benefits the employees, the managers, the organization, and especially the customers. Everybody wins with a diversity training program.

Diversity Training Promotes:

Sensitivity, Multiculturalism, Awareness, Respect, Tolerance

SUMMARY

Managing diversity is important work for the continued success of American businesses. A well-planned, strategic implementation of a diversity initiative can mean growth and opportunity. It is well worth the time, energy and resources.

Why Diversity Matters

Work with Changing Demographics

Keep Up with Federal Legislation

Prevent High Turnover of Talented Employees

Avoid Costs of Litigation and Out-of-Court Settlements

Improve Service By Capitalizing on Employees' Capabilities and Perspectives

Enhance Your Managerial Skills

Improve Your Ability to Attract and Retain the Best Talent Available

Improve Morale and Enhance Performance

Discover New Market Niches

DIVERSITY REVIEW CHECKLIST

Does Your Diversity Effort Have...

- ❑ Organizational support?
- ❑ A clear vision and mission?
- ❑ Documented organizational diversity policies and goals?
- ❑ Well-qualified and experienced diversity professionals?
- ❑ Appropriate type and length of training for audience and material covered?
- ❑ Careful attention to follow-up and support?
- ❑ Ties to other business strategies such as quality initiatives and customer service?
- ❑ Ties to economic factors?
- ❑ A budget to ensure the effort's success?
- ❑ Personal accountability?

Does Your Diversity Training Include Information About . . .

- ❑ Why management thinks diversity is important?
- ❑ How valuing diversity will increase your organization's innovation, productivity and quality?
- ❑ The current state of diversity in the organization?
- ❑ How changing demographics will affect your organization?
- ❑ What the benefits of diversity are?
- ❑ Skills for communicating when a wide range of perspectives is represented?
- ❑ How to solve problems cross-culturally?
- ❑ How people perpetuate stereotypes?
- ❑ Behaviors and languages that promote inclusiveness?
- ❑ How to develop personal action plans?
- ❑ The distribution of power and influence within organizations and society?

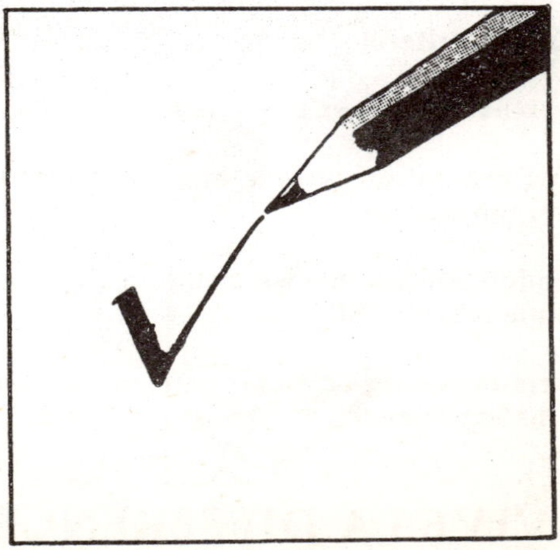

Key Learnings

- Build support for a diversity effort in the organization by sharing articles with others, especially senior managers and the human resources department.
- Attend seminars and classes that will enhance your knowledge of diversity and its applications with other initiatives like Total Quality Management.
- Contact companies with a reputation for progressive and successful diversity efforts. Identify effective strategies and obstacles they confronted.
- Include as many employees as possible in your efforts. Identify both the building blocks and the current issues.
- Link diversity with other strategies and initiatives like customer service.
- Develop a diversity-strategic business plan that outlines long-term strategies and short-term actions.
- Gain senior managements' commitment. Plan to educate them and to discuss diversity with them.
- Include measurements whenever possible.
- Clearly state success criteria.
- Use existing systems whenever possible to implement strategies.
- Build an ongoing evaluation system that will get you feedback quickly and across the organization.
- If you do not understand, or have a question about, some cultural diversity or ethnic issue—ASK!
- Remember, diversity should be about personal and organizational growth. Enjoy the experience!

VIVE LA DIFFERENCE!

BIBLIOGRAPHY

Cox, Taylor Jr. *Cultural Diversity in Organizations: Theory, Research & Practice.* San Francisco, CA: Berrett-Koehler Publishers, Inc., 1993.

Faird, Elashmawia and Philip Harris. *Multicultural Management: New Skills for Global Success.* Houston, TX: Gulf Publishing Co, 1993.

Harris, Philip R. and Robert T. Moran. *Managing Cultural Differences.* Houston, TX: Gulf Publishing Co., 1979.

Jamieson, David and Julie O'Mara. *Managing Workforce 2000: Gaining the Diversity Advantage.* San Francisco, CA: Jossey-Bass Publishers, 1991.

Loden, Marilyn and Judy B. Rosner. *Workforce America. Managing Employee Diversity as a Vital Resource.* Homewood, IL: Business One Irwin, 1991.

Simons, George. *The Questions of Diversity* (4th Ed.). Amherst, MA: ODT, Inc., 1992.

Simons, George. *Working Together: How To Become More Effective in a Multicultural Workplace.* (Revised). Menlo Park, CA: Crisp Publications, 1994.

Simons, George, Philip Harris and Carmen Vasquez. *Transcultural Leadership: Empowering the Diverse Workforce.* Houston, TX: Gulf Publishing Co., 1993.

Thomas, R. Roosevelt, Tracy Irving Gray, Jr. and Marjorie Woodruff. *Differences Do Make a Difference.* Atlanta, GA: The American Institute for Managing Diversity, 1992.

Tyler, V. Lynn. *Intercultural Interacting.* Salt Lake City, UT: David M. Kennedy Center for International Studies, 1987

Walton, Sally J. *Cultural Diversity in the Workplace.* Burr Ridge, IL: Irwin Professional Publishing/Mirror Press, 1994.

Other Media

THE INTERCULTURAL PRESS, Inc. Puts out a semi-annual catalog of books published by itself and others that are relevant to a wide variety of multicultural situations. Contact them at P.O. Box 768, Yarmouth, ME, 04096.

MULTUS, Inc., and George Simons International, *Diversophy™, Understanding the Human Race*. A training game for up to six persons using a board and cards that ask the players for facts and appropriate behavioral choices, involves them in sharing about their own background and experiences with diversity, and exposes them to the risks of working in a multicultural environment. 1993.

ODT Inc. *Diversity Resource Kit and Complete Cultural Diversity Library*. A source of articles, tip sheets, reprints, materials, and training programs on cultural diversity. Contact them at P.O. Box 134, Amherst, MA 01004.

Simons, George and G. Deborah Weissman. *Men and Women: Partners at Work*. A video/book training package including a 25-minute videotape, Trainer's Guide, and five copies of the companion book. Menlo Park, CA: Crisp Publications, 1989.

Simons, George. *Working Together: How to Become More Effective in a Multicultural Workplace* (Revised). Video/book training package including a 25-minute videotape, Trainer's Guide and five copies of the companion book. Menlo Park, CA: Crisp Publications, 1994.

YOUR FEEDBACK IS IMPORTANT

This book is the result of feedback from many clients and from hundreds of people in training workshops and seminars. Your reactions to this book are very important. Please help by answering these questions.

What was helpful about this book?

1. ____________________

2. ____________________

3. ____________________

Where can you see areas for improvement?

1. ____________________

2. ____________________

3. ____________________

Any additional comments?

1. ____________________

2. ____________________

3. ____________________

Thank you for taking the time to respond. Please mail to:

Odette Pollar
Time Management Systems
1441 Franklin Street, Suite 301
Oakland, CA 94612
(510) 763-8482
(800) 559-TIME
fax: (510) 835-8531

NOTES

NOTES

NOTES

TITLES IN THE VIVA-CRISP 50 MINUTE SERIES

ISBN	Title / Author	Price Rs. 99/- Each
	ADULT LEARNING	
— 8176495131	**Basic Business Math** by Richard P. Truchon	
— 8176495697	**Formatting Letters and Reports** by Eleanor Davidson	
— 8176496901	**Improve Your Reading Improve Your Job** by Jeanne Miller	
— 817649710X	**Study Skills Strategies** by Uelaine Lengefeld	
— 8176497118	**Successful Life Long Learning** by Robert Steinbach	
— 8176497320	**Vocabulary Improvement** by Diana Bonet	
	CALL CENTER SUCCESS	
— 8176495271	**Call Center Success** by Lloyd C. Finch	
	CHANGE	
— 8176495387	**Coping With Workplace Change** by J. Jeffreys	
— 8176495875	**Managing Change at Work** by C. Scott & D. Jaffe	
— 8176495913	**Managing Personal Change** by C. Scott & Dennis Jaffe	
— 8176497282	**Understanding Organizational Change** by L. Fossum	
	COACHING AND MENTORING	
— 8176495166	**Be Your Own Coach** by B. Braham & C. Wahl	
— 817649531X	**Coaching and Counseling** by Marianne Minor	
— 8176495328	**Coaching for Development** by Marianne Minor	
— 8176495859	**Making the Most of Being Mentored** by Gordon F. Shea	
— 8176495999	**Mentoring** by Gordon F. Shea	
	COMPLIANCE	
— 8176495522	**Disaster Preparedness** by J. Freestone & R. Raab	
	CONFLICT RESOLUTION	
— 8176495883	**Managing Disagreement Constructively** by Herbert S. Kindler	
	CREATIVITY	
— 8176495417	**Creative Decision Making** by H. B. Gelatt	
— 8176495425	**Creativity in Business** by Carol Kinsey Goman	
	CUSTOMER SERVICE	
— 8176496839	**A Positive Guide to Superior Service** by William Martin	
— 8176495018	**Beyond Customer Service** by Richard F. Gerson	
— 8176496863	**Calming Upset Customers** by Rebecca Morgan	
— 8176495441	**Customer Satisfaction** by Dru Scott	
— 8176495921	**Managing Quality Customer Service** by William B. Martin	

ISBN	Title / Author	Price Rs. 99/- Each
— 8176495972	**Measuring Customer Satisfaction** by R. Gerson	
— 817649691X	**Most Customer Services Start With the Telephone** by Nancy Friedman	
	ELECTRONIC COMMUNICATION	
— 817649738X	**Writing Effective E-Mail** by Nancy Flynn	
	FINANCE	
— 8176495050	**The Accounting Cycle** by J. Jacquet & W. Miller	
— 8176495855	**Basics of Budgeting** by Terry Dickey	
— 8176495689	**Financial Analysis** by J. Gill & M. Chatton	
— 8176496987	**Personal Financial Fitness** by Allen Klosowski	
— 817649707X	**Starting Your New Business** by Charles Martin	
— 8176497290	**Understanding Financial Statements** by James Gill	
	HIRING AND MANAGING	
— 817649500X	**50 One-Minute Tips for Recruiting Employees** by Hayes & Ninemeier	
— 8176494526	**50 One-Minute Tips for Retaining Employees** by Hayes & NInemeier	
— 8176495034	**About Pay** by James F. Carey	
— 8176495115	**Attacking Absenteeism** by Lynn Tylczak	
— 8176495174	**Behavior-Based Interviewing** by Terry Fitzwater	
— 817649559X	**Effective Recruiting Strategies** by R. Visconti & M. Brounstein	
— 817649562X	**Employee Suggestion Systems** by C. Martin & R. Bassford	
— 8176495751	**High Performance Hiring** by Robert Wendover	
— 8176496995	**Personnel Testing** by John Jones	
— 8176497037	**Quality Interviewing** by Robert Maddux	
— 8176497045	**Recruiting for High Performance** by Robert Wendover	
— 8176497363	**Writing a Human Resources Manual** by S. Brock & S. Cabbell	
	INCREASE EMPLOYEE PERFORMANCE	
— 8176495530	**Downsizing Without Disaster** by Lynn Tylczak	
— 8176495573	**Effective Performance Appraisals** by Robert B. Maddux	
— 8176495638	**Empowerment** by C. Scott & D. Jaffe	
— 8176495743	**Handling the Difficult Employee** by Marty Brounstein	
— 8176495867	**Managing Anger** by Rebecca Luhn Wolfe	
— 8176495891	**Managing for Commitment** by Carol Kinsey Goman	
— 8176495905	**Managing Negative People** by S. Michael Kravitz	
— 8176496960	**Partners in Performance** by Tony Moglia	

ISBN	Title / Author	Price Rs. 99/- Each
JOBS AND CAREERS		
— 817649528X	**Career Discovery Program** by Elwood N. Chapman	
— 8176495409	**Creating Your Skills Portfolio** by Carrie Straub	
— 8176495565	**Effective Networking** by Venda Raye-Johnson	
— 8176495719	**Getting Hired** by Richard Pinsker	
— 8176494569	**Networking for Success** by Nancy Flynn	
— 8176496944	**Preparing for the Behavior-Based Interview** by T. Fitzwater	
— 8176497002	**Preparing for Your Interview** by Diane Berk	
— 8176497088	**Strategic Resumes** by Marci Mahoney	
— 817649741X	**Your First Thirty Days** by E. Chapman & R. Maddux	
MANAGEMENT SKILLS		
— 8176495468	**Delegating For Results** by Robert B. Maddux	
— 8176495735	**Goals and Goal Setting** by Larrie A. Rouillard	
— 8176495778	**Improving Your Company Image** by Sylvia Blishak	
— 8176495948	**Managing the Technical Professional** by Herbert Kindler	
— 8176494550	**Multipoint Feedback** by D. Jude-York & S. Wise	
— 8176494577	**Project Management** by Marion E. Haynes	
— 8176497053	**Retaining Your Employees** by B. Wingfield & J. Berry	
— 8176497126	**Successful Negotiation** by Robert B. Maddux	
— 8176497215	**The Ecstatic Buzz of Doing Business** by J. Bado & C. Ivanacic	
— 8176495808	**The Internal Consultant** by Marcia Meislin	
MANUFACTURING AND INVENTORY		
— 817649514X	**Basics of Inventory Management** by J. Viale	
— 8176495158	**Basics of Manufacturing** by J. Viale	
— 8176495182	**Benchmarking Basics** by James Patterson	
— 8176495212	**Building a Total Quality Culture** by Joe Batten	
— 8176495816	**JIT Forecasting and Master Scheduling** by J. Viale	
— 8176495379	**The Continuously Improving Self** by J. Lickson	
— 8176497258	**TQM** by JoAnn Haberer & M. Webb	
PEER RELATIONS & APPEARANCE		
— 8176495247	**Business Etiquette & Professionalism** by M. Kay duPont	
— 817649576X	**Improving Peer Relationships** by Norman Hill	
— 8176495786	**Influence** by Elaina Zuker	
— 8176495794	**Influencing Others** by William Nothstine	
— 8176495956	**Managing Upward** by Patti Hathaway	

ISBN	Title / Author	Price Rs. 99/- Each
— 8176496936	**Office Politics** by Rebecca Luhn Wolfe	
— 8176496979	**Personal Counseling** by R. Knowdell & E. Chapman	
— 8176494593	**Winning at Human Relations** by Elwood N. Chapman	
	PRESENTATION SKILLS	
— 8176495581	**Effective Presentation Skills** by Steve Mandel	
— 8176497185	**Technical Presentation Skills** by Steve Mandel	
— 8176497304	**Using Visual Aids** by C. Raines & L. Williamson	
	PRODUCTIVITY	
— 8176495085	**Achieving Results** by Lorna Riley	
— 8176495093	**Administrative Assistant** by Brenda Bailey-Hughes	
— 8176496820	**Plan Your Work: Work Your Plan** by James Sherman	
— 8176497134	**Successful Self-Management** by Paul R. Timm	
	SALES AND MARKETING	
— 8176496847	**Achieve Large-Budget Marketing Without a Large Budget** by Richard Gerson	
— 8176495204	**Building and Closing the Sale** by V. Thornton	
— 8176495263	**Business Research** by P. Timm & R. Farr	
— 8176495360	**Consultative Sales Power** by Karen Mantyla	
— 817649545X	**Dealing Effectively With the Media** by John Wade	
— 8176495514	**Direct Marketing Techniques** by Lois Geller	
— 8176495603	**Effective Sales Management** by Tom Johnson	
— 8176495964	**Marketing Your Consulting or Professional Services** by D. Karlson	
— 8176497029	**Prospecting: The Key to Sales Success** by Virden Thornton	
— 8176496774	**Sales Training Basics** by Elwood Chapman	
— 8176497339	**Winning the Inner Game of Selling** by Richard Gerson	
	SELF IMPROVEMENT	
— 8176495077	**Achieving Job Satisfaction** by Editors of Crisp Publications, Inc	
— 8176495123	**Attitude** by E. Chapman & W. Mcknight	
— 8176495298	**Clear and Creative Thinking** by Herb Kindler	
— 8176495344	**Concentration** by Sam Horn	
— 8176495433	**Critical Thinking** by Daniel A. Feldman	
— 8176495492	**Developing Positive Assertiveness** by Sam R. Lloyd	
— 8176495506	**Developing Self-Esteem** by Connie Palladino	
— 8176495646	**Ethics in Business** by R. Maddux & D. Maddux	
— 817649688X	**Finding Your Purpose** by Barbara J. Braham	

ISBN	Title / Author	Price Rs. 99/- Each
— 8176495980	**Memory Skills in Business** by Madelyn Burley-Allen	
— 8176497061	**Risk Taking** by Herbert Kindler	
	STRATEGIC DEVELOPMENT	
— 8176496871	**Competency and the Learning Organization** by Donald Shandler	
— 8176495395	**Creating a Learning Organization** by Barbara Braham	
— 8176496758	**Organization Development** by Lenny Ralphs	
— 8176496952	**Organizational Vision, Values and Mission** by Scott, Jaffe & Tobe	
— 8176497142	**Successful Strategic Planning** by Stephen Haines	
— 8176497169	**Systematic Succession Planning** by Rebecca Wolfe	
— 8176494585	**Understanding Leadership Competencies** by Guggenheimer & Szulc	
	STRESS, WELL-BEING & RETIREMENT	
— 817649593X	**Managing Stress for Mental Fitness** by M. Raber & G. Dyck	
— 8176497096	**Stress that Stress That Motivates** by Dru Scott	
	SUPERVISORY SKILLS	
— 8176495042	**Accountability** by Sam R. Lloyd	
— 8176495239	**Building Trust** by Mary Shurtleff	
— 8176495654	**Excellence in Supervision** by Rick Conlow	
— 8176495700	**From Technical Specialist to Supervisor** by Donald Shandler	
— 8176497150	**Supervising for Success** by Tony Moglia	
— 8176497223	**The New Supervisor** by Elwood N. Chapman	
	TEAM BUILDING AND LEADERSHIP	
— 8176495069	**Achieving Consensus** by Jon Scott & Eileen Flanigan	
— 8176495662	**Facilitation Skills for Team Leaders** by C. Martin & D. Hackett	
— 8176495824	**Leadership Skills for Women** by M. Manning & P. Haddock	
— 8176495832	**Learning to Lead** by E. N. Chapman & P. Heim	
— 8176494542	**Motivating at Work** by Twyla Dell	
— 8176496782	**Team Building** by Robert B. Maddux	
— 8176497177	**Team Problem Solving** by Sandy Pokras	
— 8176497312	**Virtual Teaming** by D. Jude-York & L. Davis	
— 8176497347	**Working in Teams** by Sandy Pokras	
	TELEPHONE SKILLS	
— 8176497207	**Telephone Courtesy & Customer Service** by Lloyd C. Finch	
	TIME MANAGEMENT	
— 817649674X	**Office Management** by M. Manning & P. Haddock	
— 8176496766	**Personal Time Management** by Marion E. Haynes	

Rs - 99.00

	ISBN	Title / Author	Price Rs. 99/- Each
—	8176497010	**Professionalism in the Office** by Marilyn Manning	
—	8176497231	**The Telephone and Time Management** by Dru Scott	
		TRAINING	
—	8176495026	**50 One-Minute Tips for Trainers** by Carrie Van Daele	
—	8176495352	**Conducting a Needs Analysis** by Geri McArdle	
—	8176495476	**Delivering Effective Training Sessions** by Geri McArdle	
—	8176495484	**Developing Instructional Design** by Geri McArdle	
—	8176495549	**Dynamics of Diversity** by Odette Pollar	
—	8176496898	**Graphics for Presenters** by Lynn Kearny	
—	8176497266	**Training Managers to Train** by David Hayes	
—	8176497274	**Training Methods That Work** by Lois Hart	
—	8176497355	**Working Together** by George Simons	
		VERBAL COMMUNICATION	
—	8176496731	**50 One-Minute Tips to Better Communication** by P. E. Bozek	
—	8176495336	**Communicating With Employees** by Frank M. Corrado	
—	8176495557	**Effective Meeting Skills** by Marion E. Haynes	
—	8176495611	**Emotional Intelligence Works** by M. Kravitz & S. D. Schubert	
—	8176495727	**Giving and Receiving Feedback** by Patti Hathaway	
—	8176495840	**Making Humor Work** by Terry Paulson	
—	8176495107	**The Art of Communicating** by Bert Decker	
—	8176495255	**The Business of Listening** by Diana Bonet	
—	817649724X	**Thinking on Your Feet** by Marlene Caroselli	
		WRITTEN COMMUNICATION	
—	8176495190	**Better Business Writing** by Susan L. Brock	
—	8176495301	**Clear Writing** by Diana Bonet	
—	8176495670	**Fat-Free Writing** by Carol Andrus	
—	8176496928	**Powerful Proofreading Skills** by D. Smith & H. Sutton	
—	8176497193	**Technical Writing in the Corporate World** by H. Estrin & N. Elliot	
—	8176495220	**The Building Blocks of Business Writing** by Jack Swenson	
—	8176497371	**Writing Business Proposals and Reports** by Susan L. Brock	
—	8176497398	**Writing Fitness** by Jack Swenson	
—	8176497401	**Writing That Sells** by Kathleen A. Begley	

Prices are subject to change without notice.